Hats Help

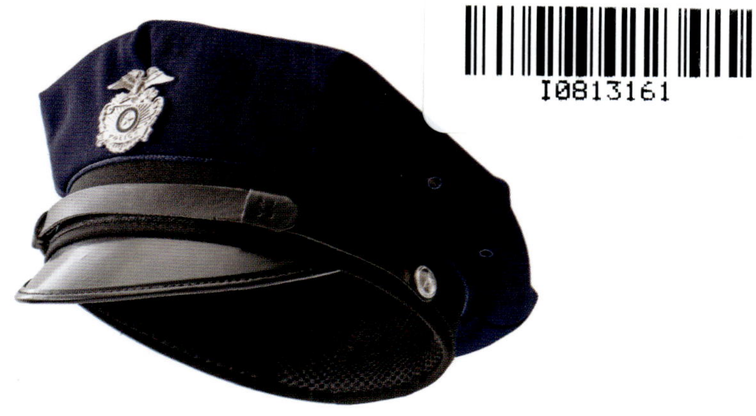

BY KIM THOMPSON

A Little Honey Book

Tips for Teachers and Caregivers

This book supports early readers as they decode words to learn facts and gain knowledge about the world.

Before reading, make sure students understand the sound-spelling correspondences shown below as well as the high-frequency words shown on the next page. Introduce the vocabulary words.

During reading, provide feedback and encouragement as students sound out decodable words by blending individual sounds.

After reading, talk about and write about the topic. Share the information on page 16 to help students learn more.

Letters and Sounds

New:

Sound	Spelling
/d/	d
/h/	h

Review:

Sound	Spelling
short a	a
/k/	c
short i	i
/m/	m
/n/	n
/p/	p
/s/	s
/t/	t

Decodable Words

can, dam, did, dim, dip, had, hat(s), hit, in, sad

High-Frequency Words

New: he, help, his, how, made, not, saw, she

Review: a, my, the, this, was

Vocabulary Words

head

kid

light

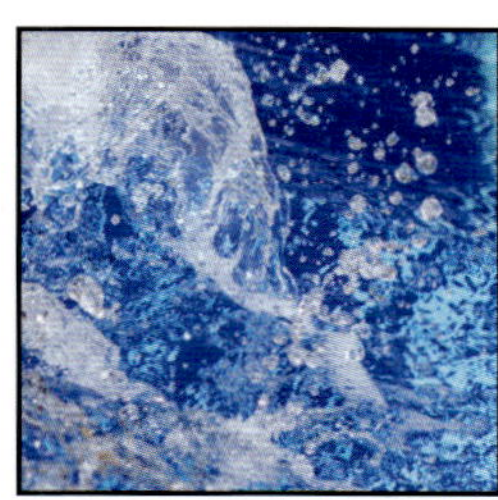

pool

Hats can help.

How did this hat help?

His **head** was not hit!

How did this hat help?

She made a dam.

How did this hat help?

He made a **kid** not sad.

How did this hat help?

He saw in dim **light**.

How did this hat help?

She had a dip in the **pool**.

How can my hat help?

Build Background Knowledge

Tools, technologies, and inventions help people get things done while staying safe. Can hats be tools? Yes! Look at the hats in this book. How does each one help solve a problem that people have? How does each one help someone do an important job or accomplish a goal? Describe the materials used to make each hat. Are they hard, smooth, electrified? How do the materials help make the hats useful tools?

Written by: Kim Thompson
Designed by: Rhea Magaro
Series Development: James Earley
Educational Consultant: Marie Lemke, M.Ed.

Photographs: All images from Shutterstock

Crabtree Publishing

crabtreebooks.com 800-387-7650

Printed in China/012024/FE20231222

Published in Canada
Crabtree Publishing
616 Welland Ave.
St. Catharines, Ontario
L2M 5V6

Published in the United States
Crabtree Publishing
347 Fifth Ave
Suite 1402-145
New York, NY 10016

Library and Archives Canada Cataloguing in Publication
Available at Library and Archives Canada

Library of Congress Cataloging-in-Publication Data
Available at the Library of Congress

Hardcover: 978-1-0398-4428-5
Paperback: 978-1-0398-4510-7
Ebook (pdf): 978-1-0398-4587-9
Epub: 978-1-0398-4657-9
Read-Along: 978-1-0398-4727-9
Audio: 978-1-0398-4797-2